Praise for Jason Ryberg

"Jason Ryberg's poetry finds, in the *dark, silent guestroom of your compounding absence,* reasons aplenty for sticking it out, for waiting for that brief, occasional epiphany that will make all life's suffering and second-guessing worth the effort. Whether it's *a sky / like a giant cut glass bowl / or classically Ptolemaic crystal sphere,* or *rain beading on the windshield / like Diamels or broken strings of costume jewelry,* Ryberg finds light refracting off some brilliant surface of the world to brighten a spot in the soul's dark surroundings. Here are sounds you never realized you'd heard: *winding / and rewinding the ancient mechanical cricket of his art, the bedside radio alarm / blows a hole in the fragile, / little submersible of your sleep,* an empty Mountain Dew bottle / sitting on a limestone post / suddenly begins to wheeze and moan / in sweet country harmony / with the wind's sad cowboy song." Join Jason Ryberg in *drifting down / a mighty Mississippi of memory.* You'll meet *this girl, / all bone and muscle / and bright blue eyes, / like windows in a tower that / should you even manage that staggering / and spiraled climb / you could probably see through time.* This book deserves a spot on your bedside table where you can follow Ryberg's advice *and read leisurely, almost Ceasarly / in languid, decadent ease.* Enjoy!"

—Roy Beckemeyer, author of *Stage Whispers*

"Jason Ryberg writes true. There is no falseness in his poetry, and that's about as big of a compliment as I can give. In this collection, you'll find excellent poem after excellent poem. Street poet? Working class poet? Ryberg is all of these and more. His words sing and howl. They are accessible in the best possible way. I'm delighted to see so much of his work together in one book. Don't pass this one up."

—Daniel Crocker, *Leadwood* (Stubborn Mule Press, 2018)

"Jason Ryberg has captured in lyrical, impassioned language, the magic, the unexpected humor (that ambushes the reader from any direction in the flyover country of the poem), the blue collar malaise and spirited intoxications that can seduce in the Great Wide Open of his inspiration. He speaks from the broad middle of the culture, Kansas and Missouri (his frequent and righteous co-conspirators), and from the broad center-stripe of his mind where the killer traffic that knows no laws, blows past on either side, its winds heralding nothing but their own subversive energies and an occasional glimpse into the oncoming, caterwauling of the near-Apocalypse. Much of his poetry is illuminated by the *nighttime world* as in this wonderful vowel-salvo from "Weathervane Creaking in a Sad, Grey Wind (or, A Secret History of the Nighttime World)," *A hobo sleeping in a rowboat/in a dried-up creek bed/beneath the white rose/of a cemetery moon.* We can assume it's the same one *tangled up among/the roots of Winter's bony, bloodless trees/where their mothers will never find them.* Ryberg's poetic macrocosm of catfish, freight trains, lone wolves, fortune tellers, weathervanes, bottom feeders and bloodhounds are not only just what they are but also represent a flotilla of other realms. Darker, deeper, more ecstatic realms that intrigue the poet with their graces as well as their arrhythmias. He writes, *Somewhere, a pay phone/by the side of a desert highway/begins to ring.* He's urging us to answer it, to imagine an America where *Somewhere, a tattoo of Chet Baker/begins to bleed.*

– John Macker, author of *The Blues Drink Your Dreams Away: Selected Poems* (Stubborn Mule Press, 2018)

LONE WOLVES, BLACK SHEEP and RED-HEADED STEPCHILDREN

POEMS (OLD AND NEW) BY JASON RYBERG

Kung Fu Treachery Press
Rancho Cucamunga, CA

Copyright (c) Jason Ryberg, 2018
First Edition 1 3 5 7 9 10 8 6 4 2
ISBN: 978-1946642-75-2
LCCN: 2018960011

Design, edits and layout: John T. Keehan, Jr.
Cover art: John E. Epic
Author photos: Will Leathem
All rights reserved. No part of this publication may be reproduced or transmitted in any form or by any means, electronic or mechanical, including photocopying, recording or by info retrieval system, without prior written permission from the author.

Special thanks to John T. Keehan, Jr, Kung Fu Treachery Press, the Black Dragon Poetry Society, The Fellowship of N-Finite Jest, The Nu Profit$ of P/o/e/t/i/c Dischord, The Osage Arts Community, Mark McClane, John E. Epic, Jeanette Powers, Will Leathem, Tom Wayne, j.d. tulloch, and the whole 39th Street School.

The author would like to thank the editors of these publications, where some of the poems in this book were previously published (in some form or another):

Gutter Elequence, Common Line Project, Downgo Sun Magazine, The Greensilk Journal, Hobo Camp Review, Lung, Lucid Moon, Rusty Truck, MiPoesias, Deuce Coupe, Falling Star, Great Midwestern Quarterly, Dream International Quarterly, Offbeat Pulp, Alternative Reel, Lit Up Magazine, Blue Island Review, Oklahoma Review, Red Fez, Eviscerator Heaven, Paraphernalia Quarterly, Killpoet, Protected: Poetry of Trains, The Smoking Poet, The Gloom Cupboard, On The Inside, Duct Tape And Coffin Nails, The Poetry Warrior, Heroin Love Songs, Debris Magazine, The Meth Lab, Clutching At Straws, Carcinogenic Poetry, Dark Lady Poetry, As Well As Magazine, Poetry Bay, pornSad, Faircloth Review, Synchronized Chaos, The Dope Fiend Daily, Punch Drunk, Trailerpark Quarterly, Ramingo's Porch, Rasputin, Mutata Re, Flint Hills Review

TABLE OF CONTENTS

A Little Too Much to Dream
  Last Night (or, Musta Thought
  It Was White Boy Day) / 1
Trouble and Desire / 4
It's Funny, the Things You Think About,
  When a Cop Puts a Gun to Your Head / 7
Jaws of Life / 10
What *It* Is (or, That's
  What I'm Talkin' About!) / 13
Generation Y Ask Y / 15
Until Further Notice / 17
The Gnome in the Corner (or,
  Pulling Weeds in the Garden
  of Earthly Delights) (Sleight Redux) / 19
Funny, How / 20
Scenes From 39th St., Pt. 1 / 23
Reconstruct / 25
One More Cup of Coffee / 28
Chicken, Matchstick-Man and Unicorn
  (or, Do Replicants Dream of Suburban
  Normalcy?) / 32
For Some Reason / 36
Loaded Dice and Poisoned Candy / 39
Never Enough to Go Around / 42
This Time / 44
How Does a Fella Get
  His Groove Back? / 46

Whereupon Jason Ryberg Very Nearly Becomes
  Another Stupid Statistic (or,
  Tonight, On Cops!) / 50
Still-life With Catfish, James Brown,
  Dragon and Freight Train / 52
20 Miles to Sturgeon Bay, Sept. 10, 2001
  (or, I've Always Wanted to Use the Line,
  It Was a Dark and Stormy Night...) / 55
Story Problem / 57
Of Kings, Priests and CEOs (or,
  Reflections on the 2008 Elections) / 60
A Better Idea / 64
The Time, Being (or *Run, Forest, Run!*) / 66
Loans, Lawyers and Lower Back Pain / 69
Constantly Flirting With Perversity / 72
The Calm Before / 75
(Otherwise) Ridiculous / 78
Everything Gonna Be All Right
  (or, Trading Body Blows With
  the Ghost of Victor Smith) / 80
Psalm #49, From *The Book
  Of Mean and Evil Truths* / 83
Horseshit and Honeysuckle (or,
  Broke Down in Kingman, Ks,
  8/14/00, 12:46pm, 110 Degrees) / 86
Ghosting Around / 89
The Problem of Desire / 91

Last Night at 4003 Wyoming / 92

Lone Wolves, Black Sheep
   and Red-Headed Stepchildren / 94

Wherein Our Hero Comes
   to the Undeniable Conclusion
   That He's Had Too Much Coffee (or,
   Meditations on Love, Sex, Death, Etc.) / 96

Writing a Poem About Smoking a Pork Butt
   in the Rain All Day While Smoking a Pork Butt
   in the Rain All Day and Writing a Poem About… / 100

On the Road with Uncle Walt and Juice Newton / 102

A Guided Tour of the Seemingly Banal / 104

Closet Full of Skeletons / Belly Full of Gin / 106

MAGA Hats Are Made in China / 107

Drunk in a Bar in Qandahar / 108

Pitchforks and Tikki Torches / 110

Uncle Mikey's Hard Night,
   Out the Door, No Time for Breakfast,
   Breakfast of Champions / 111

A Few Finer Plot Points
   You May Have Missed / 112

That Which Doesn't Kill You / 114

Integer Line / 116

Asking for a Friend / 118

This book is dedicated to
John and Melinda Ryberg.

It was a hot summer night in Mid-July,
a hangover and a black eye,
your mama said I was a loser, a dead-end cruiser,
and deep inside I knew that she was right.

-Social Distortion, *Born to Lose*

A Little Too Much to Dream Last Night (or, Musta Thought It Was White Boy Day)
with apologies to The Electric Prunes, Quentin Tarantino and Lawrence Ferlinghetti

She
    with the ab-SO-lutely hypnotic,
                interstellar-black hair
    and maliciously exposed
                    midriff
(meaning that radioactive area between,
                but also including,
    upper-most hip bone
        and lower-most rib)
                asked me to stay
    past last call, promising

    to spirit me away
        from it all (meaning, I suppose,
my otherwise meaningless life
            of de-meaning, semi-skilled toil
        and celibate drudgery)
            to some as yet undisclosed,
but no doubt, exotic locale
        for a volatile psycho /
    sexual concoction which she guaranteed
would be equal parts intensive research
        into the depths of human depravity

and dogged dedication to exhausting
······my mental,
············physical and
················moral reserves.

Whereupon, I immediately snorted awake,
············hours later,
····sprawled-out like a murder scene
··············on my living room floor,
my moment of truth
······too good to be anything but
················a cruel, booze-fueled dream,
····an alcoholic alien abduction
················leaving me bedraggled
··················and discombobulated in its wake,
························wearing nothing but
a t-shirt and a single black sock (with
················big toe protruding through
······················as if to say
····························*helllooooooo*),

····front door and fridge wide open,
················every light in the house on
····························and blazing
··············like a mid-day desert sun,

············one hand clamped on some kind of
······················suspicious-looking Dagwood sandwich,
····the other around a half-full beer,

a movie blaring out
        into the early morning dark

   for all the good people
          of the neighborhood to hear,
someone sinister saying,

        shiiit, he musta thought
                it was white boy day.
It aint white boy day, is it?

    Naw, man,
        it aint white boy day.

Trouble and Desire (Sleight *Redux*)

> Ned: *I want adventure. I want romance.*
> Bill: *Ned, there's no such thing as adventure. There's no such thing as romance. There's only trouble and desire.*
> Ned: *Trouble and desire?*
> Bill: *That's right. And the funny thing is, the minute you desire something you immediately get in trouble. And when you're in trouble you don't desire anything at all.*
> Ned: *I see.*
> Bill: *It's Impossible.*
> Ned: *It's ironic.*
> Bill: *It's a fucking tragedy is what it is, Ned.*
>
> —Hal Hartley, *Simple Men*

As it so happens,
I'm tired of thinking about things,

tired of *mulling things over*
into a flavorless conceptual paste,
tired of *thinking things through*
to their logical, but otherwise,
less than satisfying conclusions.

I've decided from now on to live my life
in the blind spot of my own mind's eye:

a compact car to a tanker
hauling liquid fertilizer
at 90-plus miles an hour.

I want to bungee from bridges
spanning unfathomable depths
of human depravity,
parachute from planes
in search of some zen-like nothingness
that comes only from risking everything
on, seemingly, nothing.

I want to conquer women with a highly potent,
yet imperceptible, synthesis of sleight of hand,
subtle hypnosis and positive / negative re-enforcement
via their own masochistic tendencies
toward low self-esteem.

I want to be mysterious, but not too threatening.
I want to be charming yet charmingly aloof.
I want to be coolly urbane yet gut-bustingly hilarious.
I want to be dangerous but sincere.
I want to be sincerely dangerous.
I want to be dangerous because I'm sincere.
I want to be a former member
of an elite, covert team of...
something or other.

I want to live a life on the run,
hitch-hike from mental state
to mental state, move from town
to no name town, always just
one step and one alias ahead of
the same mysterious (yet
oddly familiar) stranger.

I want to find the man
behind the man
behind The Man.

I want to avenge the death of my master.

I want to reel myself in
through the winding wonderland
maze of the world on a string
I left for myself countless past lives ago.

And when the great, cosmic
18-wheeler of eternity
finally comes for me
out on that lonely, moonlit
two-lane highway of Time,

will I be the lordly bull-moose
of a thousand campfire stories
suddenly appearing in the headlights,
refusing to give ground,
or a mere moth of a thought
caught in its gnarled grill,

for some higher power type character
to power-wash off later

without a second's thought?

It's Funny, the Things You Think About, When a Cop Puts a Gun to Your Head

The wings of jungle birds
and butterflies the size of catcher's mitts,
fluttering and flapping all around me
in this dream I once had where
I'm standing in a clearing in the middle
of some jungle, somewhere, beneath a sky
like a giant cut glass punch bowl
or classically Ptolemaic crystal sphere,
the sun, the clouds, the stars and moon,
each fixed in their proper place
in the grand arrangement of things,
all rolling, mechanically, over me,
down and under, back up and over,
again and again.

The wind like summer's own breath smelling faintly
of cut grass, chlorine and coconut oil (no other
collusion of smells so mutually and perfectly
complementary for pulling up so many memories,
so much of that deep down, body and soul type ache
from so far down in the well).

Or, that time Tato and I drove a load
of antique furniture to Neah Bay, WA
(the northwestern-most point of the U.S.,
by the way) and it's storming, off and on,
all the way along this winding two-lane coastal road,

and the wind is beating the crap out of the truck,
and the rain is beading on the windshield
like Diamels or broken strings of costume jewelry,
refracting the headlights of oncoming cars
into a million tiny rays, the preacher on the radio
shouting *for I am the light, I am the way!*

The dark, silent guestroom
of your compounding absence
collapsing ever-inwards upon its
no-thing-ness, its just-not-there-ness
ever since you skipped town that day.
Jesus, has it been two summers, already?
Where were you, when I needed you, baby?
What are you doing these days and is he or she
(whoever they are) keeping you happy?

And, for some reason ... stones
(somehow like the skulls of sad, hobo clowns
who dreamed, foolishly, of being poets,
of all things) sleeping underground,
now and forevermore, through the slow
rotation of the seasons.

Do they still dream down there and if so,
what do they dream of (now and forevermore,
or, until some supreme being (or next closest thing)
finally decides to stop the whole show,
in much the same way, maybe, that someone
might put a gun to someone else's head)?

Down there beneath a thick blanket of snow
and a sheet of leaves, down there beneath the soles
of my and this cop's shoes and the cold, unfeeling glare
of a phosphorescent moon, tangled up among
the roots of Winter's bony, bloodless trees
where their mothers will never find them.

Jaws of Life

You know,
maybe we should
only do unto others
as we would have them
do unto us and maybe
he or she who has the gold
does indeed make the rules
for the rest of us and I suppose
some of us should probably
try a little bit harder not to
stare at beautiful body parts
(no matter how sweet-weeping-
Jesus-on-the-cross-ly beautiful
they are) and maybe we should,
for the most part, keep our hands
to ourselves and wash them
regularly as well as brushing and
flossing our teeth daily
and not sayin' nothin'
if we got nothin' nice to say
and there's really nothin' much
you can say against the ideas
of counting your blessings
and saving your pennies

and cutting your losses
and callin' it even
and even that one about
running with scissors
is a pretty good one.
And especially that one
about not killing, but instead,
loving thy neighbor (as best as
thou possibly can without getting
thy-self steeped too deeply
in thy neighbor's business)
and not coveting or begrudging him
all his expensive stuff and / or
his hot-ass-pie of a girlfriend
or wife (not her exactly,
but one almost like her, right?)
Maybe even that one
at the bar the other night,
the one that kept catching you,
all stupid-drunk and stoned,
staring at her tits because
you couldn't bear
to look her in the eye,
couldn't stand to have her
look right through you
in that way they do
that pretty much says
they don't even see you.

Probably safe to assume,
in the end, the only one truth
that really adds up to a good goddamn
is the hard brick wall of a fact
that every morning we must rise
Lazarus-like from the beds
that we make each night,
put on our boots and our hats,
get a good running start
out the front door and dive
into the great,
wide-open jaws
of life.

What *It* Is (or, That's What I'm Talkin' About!)

It's a black feather from the wing
of a naughty Halloween angel.

It's the hot, boozy breath of Kansas;
early evening, late July.

It's flashing red lights waiting for us at the end
of the underground Chunnel of Lust.

It's the compounding absence that so often
facilitates the eye's reckless wandering,

the drunken sleep of reason
breeding monstrous nightmares
and wicked hangovers of feeling,

the darkness of the deep
Missouri backwoods after sundown
and cellars in abandoned houses
on the edge of town.

It's that high-test grade of silence
that deadens whatever meaningful
thought and speech that might
feasibly arise between us.

It's the fabled philosopher's stone in the soup.
It's bones hauled up from the bottom of a well.
It's snow in the desert (like you would not believe).

We're talking about kickin' the front door in.
We're talking about takin' the back door out.
We're talking a little *body and blood of the Lord,* baby.
We're talking dreams that sparkle and shine
like a tinfoil sculpture or a Roosevelt dime,
like the Czar's crown jewels,
scattered and sewn
out into the backyard
late one night,
like seeds,
like stars,

so they might take root
and grow into whatever it is
they were meant to be.

We're talking about that half-empty glass
of water you brought me

when you know I asked
for gasoline.

Generation Y Ask Y

Oh, by the way,
I ran into an incarnation
of the Buddha the other day
(and a truly strange variation, I gotta say),
with a mile-high pompadour,
razor-sharp chops and wrap-around shades.
He was comin' out of Dave's Stagecoach Inn
as I was walkin' in like it was fate that
we were somehow supposed to meet, there-in,
('cause I could see it in his eye
and I could tell he could see it in mine).
So, I said I'd been contemplating, lately,
the idea of entering a monestary,
at which he smiled, placidly, in that placid,
all-knowing Buddha sort of way, and asked me
why, to which I artfully parried with *perhaps
you could first provide an example of what
a proper response might sound like* but he just replied
with *there are no proper or improper answers,
only the questioning and the answering,*
to which I then said, *purple,*
at which he smiled again and, with what I'd swear
was a tear forming in the corner of his eye, said,
very wise, little cricket, very wise.

So, of course I shot him where he stood
(you know, just to watch him die),
the Great Modern American Mantra repeating
happily ever after in my mind:
Why ask why,
why ask why,
why ask why?

Until Further Notice

Seems like nothing productive
ever gets done on days like today
(not without a costly uphill battle, anyway),
here in this Any Ugly Cow Town, U.S.A.:
mid-July, no wind and 97-plus degrees in the shade
and God's murder-red eye cocked and burning at us
in such a way as to suggest he's been having second
thoughts about the human race (if not all of creation).
Meanwhile, cars continue to zoom their fleshy,
semi-sentient contents from one climate-controlled
environment to another, buses barrel and
bounce along on fluffy clouds of diesel fumes
and pedestrians do the heat stroke zombie shuffle
up and down the street, hoping to find that one
retail purchase that puts it all into perspective.
In other words, nothing much is happening
(at least not in the immediate vicinity of *yours truly*),
certainly no sexual or romantic intrigue to speak of,
no unforeseen meeting of great minds,
no major contributions to, or advancements of,
the arts and / or sciences on our part (those of us
who've somehow managed to find ourselves
(and each other) in this mercifully cool,
night-dark bar in the middle of the afternoon).

Probably safe to assume (so we might as well
get used to it), until further notice, there will,
most likely, be no retying knots that
should have been left untouched,
no putting the fallen baby bird of our lives
back in its nest.

The Gnome in the Corner (or, Pulling Weeds in the Garden of Earthly Delights) (Sleight *Redux*)

Here, inside the wire-mesh margins of the lush, overflowing Garden of Earthly Delights, one has to wonder, sometimes, whether there can possibly be a more maddeningly torturous plight (albeit, of the more gardenly varietal type) than finding yourself in over your head in some little social terrarium full of burstingly ripe nymphs and naiads, who, no matter what you say or do, cannot hear or see or, in some other way, get a feel for you, *or,* those very same nymphs and naiads very obviously in the company of various garden variety sorts of newly moneyed new-world orderlies and alpha white knights and future provider types that, in every conceivable way, appear to be the very antithesis of you. And you know exactly what they'll all be doing later don't you, you silly, little garden gnome, you (that thing that sets you to thinking and drinking too much until you swear you're gonna crack in two) when they've all finally paired (and maybe even tripled) up and gone home and there's just the moon, the garden and you? And the only thing that could possibly be even less relevant than the noxious weeds of a lonely garden gnome's quasi-poetic self-pity (that is, to this new world order) is the strange, wild flame of a flower sprouting from a crack in the head of that very gnome, sitting all alone in the corner.

Funny, How

things can so easily go sideways sometimes
and just when you start to think they might actually

be functioning properly, for once (pistons firing /
planets aligned / trains of thought, word and deed

running, more or less, on time / etc.), just when
you start to see some kind of decent, respectable

return on your investment (be it financial, psycho-
logical, romantic or some combination thereof)

some unforeseeable monkey of the perverse
(let's just say, for the sake of illustration,

outfitted with cowboy hat, bandana and
western-style vest and riding a Catahoula

Leopard Dog (oh hell, why not?)) suddenly
comes along to throw a big, greasy wrench

into the delicate Swiss watch works of your
latest machinations (be they financial,

psychological, romantic, whatever, blah blah blah).
Out there, in the wide open, wind-swept middle

of one of those moments, *motherfucker* is a word
that often comes to the mouth before it passes

the mind's inspection. *Goddamn* is another.
Son-of-a-bitch a commonly used phrase, as well.

Probably best to take it on the heel and toe, though,
before you draw any more unwanted attention

to yourself. And, of course it won't be long, now,
before you're into your fifth or sixth double gin and

tonic in some noisy midtown bar, ranting and raving
to anyone who'll listen (the girl working there

having heard it all before). Maybe you've even
managed to gather a crowd unto you (though

you're beginning to sense, somehow, that they're
laughing more at you than with you) and the jukebox

is boom-boom-booming out tune after tune
designed specifically for that pop-savvy demographic

made up, almost exclusively, of teenage girls
and thirty-something gay men and that's when

you find that you seem to have slipped
into some little isolated pocket or bubble

in the space / time continuum and you're thinking
to yourself how you'd just rather be somewhere,

anywhere else other than here: maybe on top
of a mountain or on a beach, somewhere, or even just

leaning back on the hood of your car, parked off to the
side of a country crossroads, looking up at the stars,

10 pm or so, a six pack of Mickey's, maybe,
some Chuck Berry or Buddy Holly or some of that

Beggar's Banquet or *Sticky Fingers*-era Stones (or all
of the above) on the radio and then BAM!,

you're back, just as suddenly as you left (however long
ago) and you're not sure who these people are

or how you even got there and then some slick,
wise guy playboy type with absolutely perfect hair

tells you that you're funny.
Funny?

Funny, how?

Scenes From 39th St., Pt. 1

The **Poet With The Hole In His Throat**
was busy soaking copies of *Black Like Me*
in gasoline, shouting *I told you crackers
what I'd do the next time I saw one of these things!*
And the **Eastern Academic Elitist Poet**
(from (eastern-most) Hoboken) was
attempting to set Tennyson's *The Charge Of
the Light Brigade* to Jew's harp, tone box and oboe.
And the ferocious **Celtic / Valkyrie Poet**
was feasting on the still-beating hearts
of all the fallen poets foolish enough
to have fallen for her Celtic siren song.
And **God's Angry Poet** was casting out
the under-cover **Homeland Security Man**
with Lillies of the Field and various
lyrical incantations and the street preachers
were ladeling snake oil from a fifty-gallon drum
while some faintly unwholesome character
claiming to be the latest incarnation of the Bodhisattva
was saying to everyone and anyone on the street
HEY, PULL MY FINGER! PULL MY FINGER!
And then the ten-thousand myriad archetypes
became strangely quiet and still, the stars all stopped,
momentarily, in their places and the angels
and demons ceased their square-dancing on the heads
of pins and ten-penny nails, everywhere.

And still the **Lonely Backwoods Bukowski-Wanna-Be Poet** sat there in a dank sub-basement corner of his imagination, mindlessly ringing wind chimes made from Chinese throwing stars, winding and re-winding the ancient mechanical cricket of his art.

Reconstruct
for the Little Sparrow of 39th Street

Some people
                                 seriously need to step back
and re-evaluate
                their bass
                         -ackwards social fetishes
     and faux pieties
              (always riddled, it seems,
with more than
                  the daily recompensable allowance
     of escape clauses,
                  hypocrisies and circularities
necessary to maintain
                  something even close
      to resembling a consistent
                  moral continency);
specifically, that demographic
                  that identifies itself (profusely and
ad nauseam-ly) as being
                  the biggest sky cult / death cult
on the block, endowed
                  with hugest, most massive
     divining rod and
                most righteously and
                         priapically engorged

                              with the divine right
            to lay hands upon
                        who and whatever it so deems
                as fallen and thereby falling
                                        under its dominion
and domain (which
                    pretty much includes
    everyone and everything) as well as being
                most morally fit
                            to ladle out
the healing blood
                        and sweetbread stew
rendered from one
                        of the many one true gods
        available
                to the terminally fearful and
estranged of the earth.
                        And all
        with which to more efficiently
                                    demonize,
            dehumanize
                        and goddamn themselves
and each other, respectively,
                            to the unconscionable
                and unthinkable
                                life sentence
of a life crippled and traumatized by

    the violent anti-
                intellectual insemination
of the virulent seed
            of guilt and eternal
     suffering (as in forever
          and ever without end, amen)
for such abominable and
               cosmic offenses as lust,
      masturbation and adultery.
Really,
      why don't all you little hall-monitors
            just repent, reboot
    and reconstruct,
           you sick
                  fucks.

One More Cup of Coffee
-with apologies to Bob Dylan

The day starts with a bang
as the bedside radio alarm
blows a hole in the fragile,
little submersible of your sleep
with one more report (in a seemingly endless
series of reports) about a seemingly endless
supply of bombs, of which at least one more
has gone off in a mosque or market place
or public square somewhere in a faraway land
where the very cradle of civilization
is said to have once been, and continues
to be rocked, endlessly, it would seem,
by hot desert winds made all the hotter and meaner
(if not full-on Old Testament-ly wrathful-like)
by all those bombs and various other ordinances
constantly going off (as well as the general,
over-all exhaust and roar of the Great American
War Machine doing its *business as usual,
invasion and occupation of a foreign,
sovereign state* thing).

And back here on the home front,
we've rolled up our sleeves and hiked up
our britches as we all pitch in to do our part
for the post-war, *Mission Accomplished*
phase of the operation by continuing
to borrow and spend, consume and purge
at a here-to-for unheard of and unprecedented rate,
which is maybe why even some of those
state sanctioned think tanks are starting to say
that there's probably going to be a few less
haves for the next couple of years
and a few more *have nots*.

But hey, let's not over-extend our speculations
and estimations of possible outcomes too far,
'cause back here on the home front,
maybe even a little farther inland, still,
at the over-worked, poorly maintained heart
of the Heartland, the back-rent is lagging
farther and farther back and the front-rent
is a gleam on the horizon.

And you're into a couple people
for a couple hundred bucks
and maybe there's been a medical bill or two
as well as a few other unforeseen
financial / psychological burdens.

And it surely can't help that you're living
in a city sorely lacking in love (for a fella
that's just a little down on his luck, anyway).

And sometimes it seems if it weren't for bad luck
there wouldn't be much luck to speak of
'cause there's just no decent jobs out there
these days that don't require some kind of pedigree
or credit check or Big Brotherly certification.

And, no matter what those government stooges say
or how much money the top whatever percent
is making, the goddamn economy has gone to hell.

And the weather outside is, well… frightful —
cold, wet and grey, the clouds hanging
all ominous and low, throwing down
a mean, stinging sleet that the guy on the radio
says is building up to a nice, solid sheet
of tail-bone-cracking ice on the sidewalks and streets.

So, you loiter in the shower just a little while longer,
hoping the water and steam might possibly
warm your soul a few more degrees
closer to the idea of going out into it all.

You gobble up a handful of vitamins
and maybe half a bagel or piece of toast,
throw back a shot glass of apple cider vinegar and honey,
and maybe you pour a little brandy in your next
cup of coffee and roll your first cigarette of the day
while you listen to a song about some other guy
having one more cup of coffee (and, you can probably bet,
another cigarette, too) before he, like you,
must eventually, inevitably go
out and down into the valley
of the world below.

Chicken, Matchstick-Man and Unicorn
(or, Do Replicants Dream of Suburban
Normalcy?)

You have suddenly returned
from another strange
foreign film of a dream
(of a life of suburban normalcy,
of all things)

only to find yourself (this time)
to be the sole proprietor of an illegal speak-easy,
an elegant bar in a haunted hotel
or maybe a swank nightclub in some exotic
Middle-Eastern city.

There's the grinning ghost of a bartender,
the dapper phantom of a waiter,
the wise and loyal doorman
and the lone customer (slowly
being lowered by unseen forces
down into the bottomless well
of alcohol and madness).

In the back room,
an unmanned projector
is playing the same dirty movie
over and over (the old, silent one
with all the really good parts cut out).

Maybe an idealistic, young poet
or fearless and fabulously handsome
and urbane leader of some underground
resistance movement (or some other type
of martyr to lost causes) is hiding out
in one of the empty rooms upstairs (maybe even
the one where the *unfortunate incident*
occurred last year) while someone (or thing)
even more unsettling sleeps in the basement
during the days.

You cater to an elite demographic of socialites,
sociopaths and wiseguy wannabes,
old-school drunkards and new-world samurai,
art school Muppets and indie-rock sock monkeys,
and your only real competition is a dance club
across the street, run by a shady pair of demons
named *Scratchmo* and *Sniffy*.

And it's way into the afterhours now
and you're the only one still around
and you're deep into a bottle of grappa or chartreuse
(or some other variant of industrial-strength
cleaning product).

And over in the corner, a player piano
clankity-clanks away on some ancient,
unrecognizable echo of a tune.

And the moon is peering in at you
and someone has been leaving you
strange little anonymous gifts —

a tiny chicken made from a chewing gum wrapper,
a man whittled from a single Blue Tip match
and a unicorn folded from a receipt
for Chinese takeout,

an origami unicorn that, for some reason,
seems to be more than just
an origami unicorn.

So, who is it, exactly, you've
stayed up this late waiting for, tonight
and every night, for who knows how long?

Surely not that smoky,
back roads cat of a gypsy girl,
to suddenly come calling?

Or your oldest, brightest flame, maybe,
to finally come crawling back to you
through all the highway wreckage of the years?

Or maybe you're waiting
(along with all the other sad-sack chumps out there)
on some messiah-type character
or mystified guru dude to make some kind
of big-budget Hollywood entrance

with the keys to Shiva's hoopty in one hand
and the teacher's edition of *Life's Big Book
of Mysteries* in the other (you know, the one
with all the answers in the back?).

Or maybe it's the legendary
Witness Relocation Man
and his elite tactical unit
of make-over and clean-up technicians
coming to spirit you away
to your new identity,
your newly re-revised history,
your brand-new life, overflowing
with excitement and adventure,
complete with spotless credit report
and complimentary suitcase full of cash,
personal trainer,
new car,
new house,
new face,
perfect teeth,
perfect chest,
perfect biceps,
more hair,
more time,
more life?

Not likely.

For Some Reason

The night sky is alive tonight
with glittering Diamels
and chittering super-strings
of crickets,

like sleigh bells, almost,
with their near-hypnotic ringing.

And the shadows thrown
from streetlamps are teeming
with these freaky hybrid angel / demon things.

And me, I'm whistling *Do Wah Diddy* in the dark,
stumbling, half-blind, through a graveyard
on my way home from the bar.

And the trees are whispering the latest news
and the grass is strongly advising me to
just lay down and relax.

But hey, there's no time for that
'cause somewhere, out there tonight,
there's a pale, wing'd horse on someone's roof
hoofing out the secret code
for the answers to all our troubles
(or, maybe just the winning lotto numbers).

And there's a weaselly little rat-man
in a long, black coat and top hat
sniffing and prancing about the intersection
of Bedlam and Squalor, calling out,
children, I have lollipops, children!

And a wolf in hobo's clothing
is standing at someone's sub-suburban back door,
inquiring, sheepishly, about a billy goat
or *chosen one* or somethin',

and a sad, sad boy is singin' a curbmouth blues
about a crown that's been seized
by a new king of fools.

And, for some reason, I'm seriously feelin'
like I'm about to be on the business end of some kind
of low-to-mid-level divine judgment (for something
I'm not sure I even did) manifesting itself, maybe,
as a low-hanging tree limb or slavering set of jaws
charging wildly from out of the dark or old-school
locker-room towel-snap of enlightenment
from The Almighty, Him Self.

And He's urging all His angels and demons alike to
engage target with extreme prejudice!

'Cause the word flittering, moth-like,
through the trees this evening has it that
the Moon has put a price of thirty silver pieces
on all our fool heads...

those who would dare wander
into her dark garden

without some secret intrigue
to be party to

or some mysterious stranger
to kiss.

Loaded Dice and Poisoned Candy

Hardly even know it's there
most of the time...

after all, we can be a (somewhat)
fundamentally oblivious species:

whether posited, serenely, in proper lotus position
in the middle of some shimmeringly pristine
mountaintop scenario or deeply steeped
in some sweaty, chaotic configuration of love,

or (just as likely), broke down
on the side of the highway,
I-35 let's say, just south of Topeka, Kansas
(with five pallets of National Enquirers,
bearing the tear-streaked face of Britney Spears,
that has *GOT* to get through):

a weathered cargo ship
run aground under a brutal, relentless sun,
a hundred-and-one in the shade
and a beer can rolling along all of a sudden
like a tumbleweed in an old cowboy movie,
(and now a dog barking off in the distance,
as if on cue).

So, we are allowed, now and then,
an absolution, of sorts,
from our inherent obligation
to fundamental attentiveness
to most of the obvious
and at least some of the finer points
of the subtext, metatext and copious footnotes
to the post, post-modernist novel of *Life*.

But, still *it* hovers and circles,
always lurking just out of the corner of the eye,
waiting for the perfect opportunity to strike,
doling out fate and fortune,
good, bad and indifferent, alike:

the free-floating nucleus
of the all-encompassing,
all-permeating physics of context,
the fluid matrical mechanica
of how things really are:
the constantly shifting locus
of the very *shit* that happens to us,
again and again and again
in sloppy viscous loops...

The moment ultimately coming to a point,
like the point of a big red arrow
on the Metaphysical Highway
Rest Stop Map of Life,

like the finger of God pointing,
just a little too accusingly,
at you (and you and you)
as if to say

YOU ARE HERE!

And here you are!

Hell,
everything else
is extenuating circumstances
and low-grade
accommodation,

loaded dice and poisoned candy.

Never Enough to Go Around

6am,
and the world is just about
to fire up again,

and over across the way
there's a black dog straining at its chain,
barking and barking at a starless black sky,

black sky fading to a sheet metal grey,
then, a pale powder blue,

hot black coffee starting to cool,

sixteen Redwing Blackbirds
sitting on a wire,

right above a rusted-out pick-up
that's missing its front
driver's side tire.

A shoebox full of unopened letters,

a black pleather cowboy boot
sprouting yellow flowers,

a folded piece of notebook paper,
found in a copy of *Don Quixote;*
a long list of *things to do, summer 2002*
(#14 — *Finnish Don Quixote*).

And here, at the center of it all,
an old-school, wind-up alarm clock
chopping out our meager allotments of time
with a tiny, relentless, insectile sound.

Time...

just never enough of it
to go around.

This Time

the eye of Sauron is definitely upon you,
or whatever you want to call that chilling /
crippling / just-go-limp-if-you-know-what's-good-
for-you feeling like a freeze ray or klieg light
suddenly beaming at you, prison break style,
from the dark heart of that doom-clouded
set of coordinates (just over your shoulder
and normally out of your sphere of perception
and influence); that place from where all
vaguely foreboding phone calls and
ominously certified letters seem to issue forth.
Well, at least somebody noticed your frantic,
little organ-grinder monkey antics, even if it
means your cover has been effectively blown.
Ask any sullen, scowling, chronically texting
teenager; sometimes, merely being acknowledged
by someone (anyone) is validation enough.
Other times, best to stay incognito and off the grid:
an unlisted phone number, maybe,
and a forwarding address in someone else's name,
a *cash only* policy and nothing anyone
would even think about putting a lien on.
Unfortunately, the tectonic plates of reality
seem to move with a life of their own
(and with no applicable quality even close
to resembling concern for your dumb ass);

one minute it's all champagne and chicken wings,
the next you're out the backdoor
with a suitcase in the middle of the night
and no looking back, the Polaroid snapshot
taped on the refrigerator door (you and some girl
from some long ago and presumably better time)
the only proof you were
ever here.

How Does a Fella Get His Groove Back?

Oh, it's all well and good
when the world helps a sad lady
get back on her feet again
and truly start to believe again
and laugh out loud
in the wide-open-like
-a-flower / sun is shining /
birds are singing /
outside world again,
and takes her out dancing
and buys her dinner and drinks
and shows her the glittering path
to new and fabulous romance.

But, how does a fella
get his groove back:
his moves,
his verve,
his nerve to follow through
on the follow-through?

Or, is he like a race horse come up lame
or a ball player that's lost his game,
for most intents and purposes, ruined?

That is to say,
once he starts losin'
(and losin'
and losin')
is he doomed
to keep on losin'
and with little hope
for some new precedent set
to stop his slow, grinding
wounded-submarine-on-the-side
-of-an-undersea-canyon-like descent
into the funky, foul-smelling pit
of compounded booganism?

And if (as some would say)
a man is his game,
his moves,
his groove,
and the groove
is what maketh the man,
then is a man that's lost his groove
less than a man?

Maybe a bumbling, buffoonish,
fundamentally clueless
Beaver Cleaver / Charlie Brown hybrid
kind of a man?

A mildly amusing Charlie Chaplin tramp
or Gilligan-esque court jester, always good
for a tumbling pratfall kind of a man?

Maybe a skittish little Woody Allen (without
the jokes or geeky, boyish charm) kind of man,
or a poor, little Oliver with wide, hopeful kitten eyes
and empty bowl kind of man.

A *right away, on the double, sir!* kind of man.

An *of course I wouldn't mind
dancing your Cutty and water
over to you, sir* kind of man.

A *my lord, the Royal Chef assures me
your Hasenpfeffer should be ready
any minute, now* kind of man.

And whereby and therefore (in accordance
with the universal laws of God, woman
and natural selection), should anyone
but this man's mama really even give a damn?

And once the *It*, which so vitally composes and
contributes to *The Shit* (which it seems he must
at all times and with supreme universal confidence
believe himself to be) is lost, is there really any chance
of getting it back again?

Any probability or possibility
of hope, left in Pandora's
little black grab bag,
for a monkey-boy to be a man again?

Or, is a man,
once his spirit and stature
have been sufficiently dismantled
(and the parts all sold for scrap),
best led out back behind the wood shed
or to an open pasture, somewhere,
and the fabled Diamond Bullet
of Clarity put through his head?

'Cause sometimes there seems to be
a mighty fine line between
the merely walking wounded

and the dead that just don't know
they're dead.

Whereupon Jason Ryberg Very Nearly Becomes Another Stupid Statistic (or, *Tonight, On Cops!*) (Sleight Redux)

Ever found yourself suddenly struck dumb, almost in that old-fashioned gothic horror novel sense of the term, say in the middle of a conversation about the whole art / life / truth and beauty thing with a beautiful nude girl (she having just stepped Venus-on-the-half-shell-like, out of the shower, all steamy and flowery-smelling, after some of that nasty, early-morning, barely-even-awake-type fucking), and, for some reason, you have a pair of those steel, Chinese exercise balls in your hand (you know, *cling-clang*) and maybe you were even thinking *man, you could probably dent a guy's head-bone pretty good with one of these things, if you really had to* and almost precognitively, you could say, because you're now waiting for the *reformed* skinhead who has just this instant walked into the room (and completely out of nowhere and unexpectedly, in all fairness to his stealth capabilities) to do ... something, anything but just stand there and stare (her fairly recent, on again / off again ex-boyfriend, it's safe to assume, so recent, in fact, that he may have only just recently got the news)? And CHRIST it's only 10am and it's raining outside and here we are locked in some kind of retarded three-way Mexican stand-off (wherein, did I mention, one of the parties is stark naked, for the most part, except for a towel?)

in a fourth-floor apartment (with locked front door, by the way, leaving the back fire escape and fourth-floor balcony as the only possible sources of (more than likely) forced entry for this chowderhead, this (understandably close-to-apoplectic but otherwise) sad sack chump with the classic, Hollywood-esque duh / what the fuck look of the genuinely dumbstruck; this yay-hoo, this nowheresville palooka with muddy boots and knuckle tattoos, or, as that consummate wise-guy hipster, Bugs Bunny (or was it Bugsy Seigel?), used to say, *what a maroon)*. And I'm watching him and he's watching me, then we both look at her, then back at each other and she looks like maybe she's thinking about what she's gonna wear today or what she's gonna have for breakfast later *(the banana pancakes or the Belgian waffles?)*. And he's gotta be thinking something close to what I'm thinking, which is actually something somewhere between *well, here's how it ends for old J. Ryberg, I guess* and something slightly more alpha like *this motherfucker needs to hurry the fuck up and get it over with and make a move or turn the fuck around and get the fuck outta here now!* And she just calmly (I shit you not, absolute picture of), nonchalantly says *oh, hi Chad*.

Still-Life with Catfish, James Brown, Dragon and Freight Train

> *This aint Bohemia, baby. This is skid row.*
> -Victor Smith

The walls are peeling
and the ceiling is rotting
and the clock in the corner
is chipping away at the night.

And outside, a dog is barking somewhere far off
and someone's shouting down on the street,
HEY RON! HEY RON! IT WASN'T ME, MAN,
IT WASN'T ME!

And the fan on the floor is brushing out a sultry rhythm
and the pipes are whispering all the secrets
of those who've lived here before
and the fridge is humming low,
darlin' do you remember meeee?

And the used car salesman upstairs
is laughing like a mandrill (or crying like a kookaburra),
the people next door, fighting or fucking,
through the walls it's hard to tell.

But through the unlikely collusion
of these people, this place and all the little things
randomly arranged along the winding spectrum in
between, sometimes I think some larger,
more primal thing is trying to contact me.

I have to admit,
it's hard to make out most of the time,
like there's just too much metaphysical clutter
or white cosmic noise for the message to get through.

In a painting on the wall, for instance,
a fat catfish is giving the fish-eye
to a hook and worm.

In the corner, sitting on a table,
between a jug of homemade blackberry wine
and a bowl full of nectarines,
the bust of James Brown is eying me
just a little too knowingly,
letting me know with that wicked grin of his
that he's seen everything (and that means *everything!*).

And somewhere, at the bottom
of the deep, murky gravel pit of my gut,
down among the bottles and bones,
the scuttled cars and sunken rowboats,
down among the spiky, prehistoric fish-critters
and chitinous mollusks that skulk and sniff about
in the oily dark of this forgotten underworld,
the *Duende* / dragon / angel / demon hybrid thing
they say lives inside every sensitive artiste type
is tossing and turning again,
tossing and turning, cursing his rotten luck
at having been found out again
by the only bigger and badder monstrosity
on the block than him —

this accursed, marauding insomnia
that now comes calling whenever it pleases
(yes it does, whenever it pleases!).

Though, I know he has been giving
more and more thought,
as time slowly tics and ratchets by,
to raging up in a thunderous,
locomotional flurry of fang
and claw and fire and wing
and taking a good-size chunk
out of the ass-end of the world.

Just to see the looks on all our faces.

But outside, up here on the surface of things,
beneath a neo-classical, nocturnal scene
of cirrus clouds and contrails
and a big, bright, mag-light of a moon,
a freight train bound for Talala, OK,
Tucumcari, NM, Ithaca, NY (or other
exotic parts unknown to most of us)
is rumbling its way past the building again,
shaking the very pillars of the earth
like wave after wave of armored cavalry,
rattling the aching frame of Atlas, even …

How often's it go by, man?

So often you won't even notice.

20 Miles to Sturgeon Bay, Sept. 10, 2001
(or, I've Always Wanted to Use the Line,
It Was a Dark and Stormy Night...)

and there I was,
wrestling a five-ton truck
with a fifteen-foot trailer
(and both packed tight, top to back,
I might add) down a twisting
two-lane back road (no shoulder,
no signs, no cell-phone service
for miles) way up there on
the coast of that skinny Wisconsin
peninsula that pokes so broken
pinky-like out into the black and
nebulous gloom of Lake Michigan.
But at least it was relatively
warm and dry inside the cab,
though my partner and I
were still a bit shaken and chilled
to the marrow of our respective
labor-bruised bones by the over-all
unnerving (if not full-on traumatizing)
work conditions we were then currently
enduring, as in the absolutely
merciless and insane Hollywood-style
thunder and lightning and rain (with the
occasional visitation of hail, now

and again) and damn-near zero
visibility beyond the headlight's
faint and watery glow on the treacherous,
hairpin curvature of the road ahead
and of course the odd moment of
HOLYCRAPWE'REGONNADIE!
But hey, at least we've got half a tank of gas,
half a bag of giant pretzel sticks,
a couple cans of some toxic, psychotic
energy drink rolling around, somewhere,
and ZZ Top's *Cheap Sunglasses*
is just now coming on the radio
and the sign by the side of the road
says, *20 Miles to Sturgeon Bay*
and it looks like we just might
make *last call*
with time
to spare.

Story Problem

It's that time of night again when
all the little segmented and many-legged
critters of the mind's darker side come creeping
out of their slimy little hidey-holes
and the city seems to sporadically come alive
with sirens from time to time (and then
die back down again like nothing ever happened).

And the moon is seated up there
in its royal couch of clouds,
shining like someone's back porch light
out into the summer nighttime, backyard
jungle-world of childhood (even though it's really
October 2008 as I'm writing this, way down here
at the court-side seats of the big Here and Now).

But, *that* fondly (and often rather fuzzily)
remembered time of our lives, for many of us, anyway,
has long since sailed on, out into that great, grey fog bank
of eternity (and, it's easy to think, sometimes,
the best things in this life with it (meaning, I suppose,
those moments and events and things that people
so often write children's books and memoirs and even
the odd weepy or wistful poem about)).

Yes, it's that time of night, perfect also, for otherwise
less-than-fond memories of the past (be it whatever
randomly assigned childhood or adolescent scenario
or your early-to-mid-to-late twenties or just last week,
even, for that matter) as well as those Standard Issue
Fears of the Future, that plague so many of us,
to make an unannounced appearance
(or at least their presence felt),

not unlike mice in the walls, maybe,
or the manic skitter and scurry of squirrels
in the attic or a dog out there, somewhere in it all,
that you'd swear was barking at the wind.

And the mighty I-35 continues its non-stop
guttural grumble and growl.
And the trees are scratching and tapping
at the house like maybe they were feeling around
for a way in, or something.
And tonight, it all seems to have come down
to this seemingly simple story problem:

1 last beer in the fridge,
1 inch of bourbon in the bottle,
13 (or so) minutes until the liquor store closes,
roughly 5 minutes to get there (if you go right now),
an unknown quantity (x) of the usual frisky demons
to keep you entertained for an unknown quantity (y)
of sleepless hours before you.

And of course, now, you have to factor in
how you've really been trying to cut back on it all
(the booze, the coffee, the fried food,
the staying up too late every night
just to carve these humble missives
into the sacred wood of the *uncarved block*),
get back in some semblance of shape
and back into the game
before it really is too late for you

(and, like the man said,
*aint nothin' worse
than too late*).

So,

what do you do?

Of Kings, Priests and CEOs (or,
Reflections on the 2008 Elections)

The weather channel is showing
highly detailed satellite imagery
of impending meteorological doom
while various other sources are warning
of a new ice age (and a giant meteor
thrown in, to boot),

and the street corner preacher
(in chorus with his whole inbred clan)
says *GOD HATES FAGS!* (which makes me wonder
what the big He / She / It up there in the sky
must think about rogue investment bankers,
government *interrogators* or sowers of paranoia
and discord masquerading as journalists
(or porn-addicted poets, for that matter)).

Even the usually reliable Magic Eight Ball
says, *it doesn't look good.* And, apparently,
our current (and wildly popular (if not so
genuinely populist)) Republican vice-
presidential candidate enjoys, among other things,
shooting wolves from helicopters and firing librarians
for refusing to ban *objectionable* books,
believes dinosaurs roamed the earth
six thousand years ago

and when asked in three separate interviews
what the official duties of the vice-president
of the United States of America were,
couldn't answer correctly.

Really, should this person have access
to the nuclear codes?
But the lost boys and the strippers,
the third shift factory workers and EMTs
are all finishing up their nightly routines
and waiting to get off work
and head over to Cooper's for a drink.

Thank God someone in this city
(of a hundred and thirty-one homicides
this year, and climbing)
is open at 6am.

But what was it the old boy with the cowboy hat
and Wally Walrus moustache was saying, just then:
something about the *Philosophick Mercury* or
Grand Quintessence as cosmological constant,
or something?

We can probably assume there used to be
competing schools of thought set up to address
those and other pressing issues of the day
and that there surely must be remnants of their
descendants left in the universities and non-
partisan think tanks here in our own uncertain age.

Or, maybe, when confronted
with the various cultural / quasi-intellectual
bogeys and conundrums of the modern world,
we should all just step back and calmly review
the situation and maybe think about renewing
ours vows to our estranged lover or spouse,

that He or She (or whoever in between)
of Reason and Critical Thinking,
sitting all alone at the end of the bar,
nose in a book, sipping on a soda with lime,
the one who keeps looking at you
from time to time out of the corner of their eye,
maybe even stealing a full-on glance
when they're sure you've turned away.

How is it you don't remember them
looking so damned good,
so fit, so linear and clean?

Not like the sad, flabby menagerie of crazies
and bar-whores of hysteria and misinformation
you've been truck-stopping around with lately.

How did things ever degenerate
to this sorrowful state?

How did we ever get conned
into believing we're born *fallen*
and fully deserving of a life
(and eternal afterlife) of suffering?

How do we get fooled again
and again and again into laboring
against our own best interests
and thinking that we ever had
anything to gain from maiming
and murdering each other
over the petty disputes

of kings, priests
and CEOs?

A Better Idea

Today, nothing seems to make
more sense than to sit outside
in the backyard under a tree
in a cheap folding metal chair
(that I'm pretty sure was here
when we moved in three years ago),

the classical station on the radio,
a bucket of some fancy European beer on ice,
massive clouds doing their continental drift thing
across an ultra marine blue ocean of sky,

birds and squirrels and butterflies
flittering in and out of the scene,

and maybe the unexpected appearance
of a dragonfly or big, fat bumblebee
(just to make things a little more interesting),

and nothing to do but move the sprinkler
around in the garden every twenty minutes or so,
soak up whatever piano concerto or solo for violin
they might be playing throughout the day,
drink every last one of these beers
while reading leisurely, almost *Ceasarly*
in languid, decadent ease from a tall stack
of books on the table beside me:

Whitman, Sandburg, Williams, Stevens, Rexroth,
Neruda, Langston Hughes, Ted Kooser, Harley Elliot,
Steven Hind, Charles Simic, Lawrence Ferlinghetti,
Albert Goldbarth, just a few of the old boys that first
made me really wake up and take notice and
ask of the universe, *Hey, can I play too?*

And who knows, maybe I'll eventually
get around to doing a few other semi-
productive things out here today.

Maybe take a nap later,
wake up around seven or eight,
a cup of that Zapatista medium roast
in the shower then head down
to 39th Street for something to eat.

Maybe a couple of gin and tonics
somewhere, then see if somebody
wants to sneak a pint of something
into a late movie;

I don't know,

something with
kung fu and vampires
and lots of stuff blowing up in it.

You got a better idea?

The Time, Being (or, *Run, Forest, Run!*)

> *Better get busy livin,' or get busy dyin.'*
> *God damn right.* -Irish Red

The hill has been taken
for the time being,
the flag reclaimed
and the first-born bastard child
of every household has finally returned
from his or her aimless wanderings
and night errantries abroad
(demanding parental validation
and their compounded allowance).

And the priests and politicians
and insurance salesman
are quietly slipping out of town,
and the future wives of upper-middle America
are planning weddings to men they haven't even met.

And the guards of the gated kingdoms
have nodded off at their posts again,
allowing Night and its gypsy gothic entourage
to slip right in.

And the whole slapstick, tear-jerking
tragi-comedy of it all will one day be recorded
on the walls of the deepest caves
for our great, great grandchildren
to one day find and wildly misconstrue.

And all the while, Life and Death
continue their heated Mexican stand-off
in the middle of the restaurant
while the rest of us look anxiously on,
staring into our Denver omelettes and Belgian waffles
and veggie-tofu scramblers, hoping, praying, pleading,
wishing we were having our *breakfast anytime*
any other time than this.

But really, now is probably the time
to learn to play the piano,
time to lose those troublesome twenty pounds,
time to drain the bad blood
from the abscess of the family,
to go back to veterinary school,
to come out of the closet,
to finally ask that waitress out,
to write The Great American
post-post-modern crime / noir / sci-fi novel,
time to do that thing (whatever it is)...

You know, that *thing* you go on and on about,
ad nauseum-ly, everytime you hit your requisite
number of drinks?

Seriously,
better get to it,
better get steppin,'
better come on with the come on,

'cause the time, being
what it is
(was,
will be),

won't just
wait around for you

indefinitely.

Loans, Lawyers and Lower Back Pain

We sat on the front porch,
drinking warm Lone Star
and Old Overholt Rye—

a balcony seat
overlooking late July's
flickering picture show of trees
and birds and ribbons of cloud
against a molten-silver sunset.

He talked about loans and lawyers
and lower-back pain,
how his father handed down to him
the farm and family debt,

how he was fairly sure
it was the hard life of a farmer (at least partly,
the drinking and shouting and throwing of things, aside)
that became too much for (at least) two
of his three ex-wives

and finally, how one dry, raw August day,
fifteen misplaced years of planting and selling,
struggling and saving and barely scraping by
suddenly resurfaced like a body in a lake,
a deep, dark secret no one wanted to know:

the whole ugly mess of it
seizing up into a tight constricted knot
of absolute, unflinching clarity,
and with a bang, a sputter
and one well-placed *MOTHERFUCKER!*
it all ground down to an irreparable halt.

He swears to this day
that something inside of him
broke as audibly as anything
under the hood of that truck,
leaving him, for the most part, though,
a better, happier man,

absolved,
enlightened, even,
purified by a fire
of (at least, partly) his own making.

And the old Mack?

It's still sitting there
right where it stopped,
awash in a slow tide of time
and prairie grasses,

the bed still full of compost,
compressed by the layered chemical weight
of twenty years of sun, wind and snow,

exploding each summer
into a small, dense island
of sunflowers,

the only proper monument,
you could say,

to loans,
lawyers
and lower-back pain.

Constantly Flirting with Perversity
-apologies to Lawrence Ferlinghetti

Constantly flirting
with perversity and irrelevance,
hilarity and mayhem (and whatever
other fates, furies and / or muses
that may or may not come forth)
whenever he performs
his *wickity-wack* shtick
before the giant,
disembodied bobble-heads
of the court,

the poet, like the contortionist
or alchemist (though really more like
the civil war re-enactor
or H.A.M. radio enthusiast)

must attempt to lasso the spotlight
of world opinion away from his fiercest rivals,
the Sports / Industrial Complex
and Celebrity Kulture TV (with a golden,
truth-revealing lariat of his own weaving)
and all the while trying to kick ass
and look good at the same time,
maintaining a confident smile
and not breaking a sweat or breaking
for a smoke or a piss or nothing.

For he is supposed to be
the super-duper-surrealist who must (of course)
do battle via his art with his arch-nemesis,
the man behind the man behind the curtain,
the Usurper-Realist —

he who hath conscripted and distorted
fair Truth and Beauty and pimped them out
to the lowest and meanest of common denominators
(for whatever nefarious experiments and other
lurid purposes, no doubt).

So, good people of highest, lowest
and most smack-dab in the goddamn
nowhere middle of America,
let us take a moment of silence tonight
to drink one for ambulance drivers
and elevator repairmen,
for neurosurgeons and airline pilots,
night watchmen and day laborers,
high school science teachers
and hostage negotiators,

all the Jack O' Lanterns, Wandering Jews
and Flying Dutchmen out there,
far from home and lost in the night,
keepin' it real and fightin the good fight
(or just tryin' to keep a low profile),

but, also, one for our neoclassical anti-hero, here,
this little Mighty Mouse of a character
daring to triple-dog-dare The Great Dragon
of the Airwaves (a.k.a. The Giant Spider
of the Inter-Webs) to come on down
from its top-floor office suite

and step into the ring.

The Calm Before

It's been another long and perilous week
but we've finally come around
to the relative calm of another Sunday afternoon.

And the sun has just now slipped away
behind a slate-grey bank of clouds
and the wind is still rolling around
in its dream-soaked sleep
over in the vacant, weed-clotted lot
across the street.

But the traffic 'round town
churns and lurches
and then suddenly stalls,
lurches and stalls,
lurches and stalls
all with the passive-aggressive demeanor
of massive schools of tropical fish.

And so far,
it's been another one of those
barren, bombed-out type of Sundays
wherein nothing really happens
and the weather and the time
fight a cold civil war of attrition
for a mere toehold on the day,

one of those days
when you just can't seem
to get your bearings
or screw your head on straight
or locate your proper place
in a world full of places
where you don't want to be,
people you don't want to meet
and useless things you don't need.

And all your meager thoughts
and sentences are randomly sprouting wings
(the very second they come into being, it seems)
and, somehow, the very likely likelihood
of (what in all likelihood would be)
some seriously white-hot sex is... no big thing,

and even Miles and Mingus and Monk
have, unprecedentedly,
misplaced their swing (surely
the problem couldn't be
with you or me?).

Hell, it could only mean one thing:
the clouds,
the wind,
the traffic racing aimlessly around town,
the slow stalagmitization of seconds
into minutes into hours,

otherwise known as our Indentured Servitude
to Time (otherwise known as this Post-
Post-Modern Life of Ours),

they're all larger parts of the sum
of the numb, melancholy calm
swelling before the storm
of Monday morning
comes rudely blundering in:

that vaguely ominous,
imminent negative
like an approaching tunnel
out of which
will eventually,
inevitably,
inescapably roar

a runaway freight train
haulin' in nothin'
for you, baby,

but bills,
bad attitude
and diminished expectations

of everything.

(Otherwise) Ridiculous

The lone *Bos primigenius*
on the hill at night,

do you suppose she ever wonders
in her laconic, bovine way
what the stars could possibly be?

Does the *Tyto alba* contemplate
the moon's topography (from his
hayloft perch) or what mysteries might
lie on its darker side?

The *Nephila clavata* centered
in his jeweled web,

does he receive strange frequencies
(or just old radio transmissions)
on its taut wires and filaments?

What about the sleepless *philosopher / poet*
taking his thoughts out for a late-night
walk around the neighborhood?

Does the universe leave cryptic,
fortune-cookie clues and candid
little Polaroids of the *Bigger Picture*
lying around for him to find
and piece together later?

Or is this semi-educated fool merely
adrift on a sea of his own imagining
in the leaky rowboat of his skull

and nothing
but a kerosene lamp,
a stone jug of his uncle's corn liquor
and an old typewriter on which
he may compose

such (otherwise) ridiculous
and impertinent

questions?

Everything Gonna Be All Right
(or, Trading Body Blows With
the Ghost of Victor Smith)

The night was thick, black and nasty
and my mattress was a raft drifting down
a mighty Mississippi of memory,
a Viking longboat in which my broken
warrior-poet's form had been placed
and sent downstream through the silver-grey mists
of eternity and on to the far bright shores of my
forefathers and their fathers before them,
only to be turned away from those fearsome
gates for being *insufficiently deceased.*

And, lately, it seems like I've been waking up
in the middle of varying stages of dream-state
at all my *former places of residence,* feeling around
the bed for some imaginary *former spouse
or significant other,* freaking out about
being late to some *former place of employment*
and whatever it is I'm gonna say (this time?)
to placate whichever *former employer.*

I can't help but believe if things continue
at this rate, eventually, I'll bolt awake thinking
I'm late for my first day of kindergarten (though,
hopefully my mother will also be on hand to say,
It's OK, little man. It's only Saturday. Go out and play).

And then there's that recurring one where,
in what some new age, metaphysical,
guided meditation counselor type might
call *a deep subterranean cave of me*,
some heretofore unknown (or merely suspected)
part of me suddenly cracks and snaps off
like a massive icicle or stalactite, morphing
on its way down into another more fully actualized me,
a new and improved me, you could say,
and hits the ground running like Jesse Owens
at the '36 Olympics.

And let's just say, for the sake of the poem
(and your, most likely, all-too-brief relationship with it),
that this new and improved me is actually you
and it's not a slimy or treacherous cave floor
that your feet have found but a cool, rain-slicked street
late at night in some industrial part of town
you don't recognize.

And just over there to the right,
maybe fifty, sixty feet away at most,
there's a freight train blowing out
its big, brassy *basso profundo*
as it slows down to take the curve
and it's not even an issue of nerve
or wanting it bad enough 'cause you know
you can make it this time, man,
and you don't even have a suitcase
or bag or nothing,

but that shit don't even matter 'cause everything's
gonna be different from here on out if you can
just catch that train, man, everything gonna be just fine
if you can just keep runnin' and sayin' it
and sayin' it and sayin' it:

everything gonna be all right,
everything gonna be all right,
everything gonna be all right,
everything...

Psalm #49, From *The Book
of Mean and Evil Truths*
for Josh Rizer

One day,
sooner or later,
you will begin to see it:

a memo from the main office
appearing, intermittently, in the classifieds,

on billboards next to highways,
subliminal transmissions
insinuated into the continuum
of prime-time television
and late-night radio programming,

as public service announcements
between infomercials at 3am:

*please find something constructive
to occupy your time.*

Street cleaners and heads of state,
drunken painters, relocated witnesses
and wizened philosophs,
they'll all confirm the urgency
of these instructions.

For they too have seen (if but
in their magically realistic dreams, at least),
the Cosmic Steel Toed Boot come swinging.

They know that should you maintain
your current state of in-action,
your current holding pattern of bad faith,
one day, with a long, running start
and supreme universal indifference,
your sweet ass will surely be kicked
right out of the world.

No, not into the void or the here-after, exactly,
not prison or the escape velocity
necessary to achieve a truly perfect madness
(or even the dreaded de-classification
unto the Great American Underclass)...

but a fate far worse
from which few ever
manage to dig themselves out,
like the final scene from one of those bleak,
existential French or Swedish cinematic dirges
forever looping and repeating itself
again
and again
and again...

The Great Feast in the grand,
Ayn-Randian dining hall
of the Immortals.

A rickety folding table
set for you in the corner.

A place-card with your name on it
(misspelled, of course).

And there you are,
reeling at the crosshairs of it all,

the guest of the guest of the Guest of Honor,

your demeanor, somewhere between
a boxer's permanent punch-drunk
and low-grade PTSD.

And all the food and booze is gone
and all the lights are out
(except for one dirty bulb
above the sink).

And everyone else
has paired (and even tripled) up
and gone to bed.

And the walls

are thin,

fucko.

Horseshit and Honeysuckle
(or, Broke Down in Kingman, KS,
8/14/00, 12:46pm, 110 degrees)

There was this girl,

all bone and muscle
and bright blue eyes,
like windows in a tower that,
should you even manage that
staggering and spiraled climb
to look out from them,
you could probably see through time.

And we're all just standing in line
at the auto parts store
in downtown Kingman, KS,

12:46 pm, a hundred-and-ten degrees in the shade
and birds are droppin' from the trees
and people are wandering the streets like zombies,
begging for a kind and loving god to strike them down
right there where they stand.

But there's this girl, see,
and she's holding a solenoid
or water-pump or somethin', I don't know,
'cause I don't wanna get caught
checkin' her out, ya know.

And she has this prairie fire mane of red hair
that can only be described as *leonine*
(a rather antique term, for sure,
but the only one that really nails it).

And her eyes, people,
her eyes are blue halogen headlights
illuminating a lonely room at midnight
and she looks and smells so damn good, man,
it hurts; I mean it fucking *hurts*.

And she's standing right there,
an earth-bound goddess waiting in line
like everyone else,
smelling like flowers
and wild blue yonder,
about to burn Kingman, KS
off the ass-end of the earth
like a bad tattoo.

And it's been damn near ten years, now,
and of course I never got her name,
never even saw her again even though I spent
that whole summer hitting every bar and roadhouse
within fifty miles of that town.

And she's probably married with kids
and pets and a big, yellow HUMV
(with a McCain / Palin sticker on it, no doubt)
in some sub-suburban cul-de-sac
or terrace somewhere...

But, for exactly ten seconds that day,
I couldn't remember my address,
my own phone number
or any of the horseshit
and honeysuckle
I'd ever called
poems.

Ghosting Around

Tonight,
the sky
is a scarifying movie

and my head
is an empty doll house
(wherein all its (former?)
occupants
are dead).

Yet, instead
of lying quietly
in their places
in the dark
and wormy
Deep
Down,

all these shapes
and faces
keep on bumping
and billowing
and ghosting around
in here somehow.

Yep, there's always
chains a-draggin'
way up there in the attic

where all the leather of bats
and feathery flaps
of crows
are stowed.

Then there's the groanin'
and moanin'
(at two or three
in the mo'nin')
down there in the basement
where the lizards
and crickets
and toads
all go.

And up
and down the stairs,
at rhythmically
confounding intervals,

up and down
the stairs

(sometimes in triplets and pairs),

someone's feets
go stomping

and

clomping.

The Problem of Desire (Sleight Redux)

(Buddhist maxims aside), that is of wanting something bad enough (maybe even above all else in life), say to the point of convincing yourself over a long enough period of time that this thing you desire is actually a necessity for life (or better living, at least) and, who knows, it may well be but still, the fact is that, more often than not, it seems to be compounded, inversely, almost exponentially, even, by the inability (for whatever reasons) to obtain or attract that very thing you so desperately, tragi-comically, (aint-it-a-goddamn-cryin'-shame-fully) burn for, leaving you, for the most part, out in the cold, as they say, looking in on life's great feast (Joyce, maybe? or Cab Calloway?), all dry-mouthed, heart pounding and short of breath, a near-constant, agitated state of desperate neediness mixed with some sort of sub-Shakespearean grade of thwarted ambition and good, old unrequited lust (who knows, maybe even love). Chances are you'll drink some out there (most likely, a little more than you would otherwise), probably even smoke a little weed and snort up a little coke (both likewise: *see above*). Or you might take up hunting or civil war re-enacting or throw yourself, completely, into one or more professional sports teams (of course, only in the passive / aggressive observer capacity), comic book or record collecting, pornography and / or video games, sacrifice yourself (headfirst) to some wacky bronze (or new-) age religion, submerge and re-submerge yourself in book after book after book about ... anything, everything, nothing. Who knows, you might even try writing poetry.

Last Night at 4003 Wyoming

May 1st, 12:20am
and here I am kicking back
on this rickety wooden chair,

like some kind of lazy, post-post-modern
beatnik cowhand after a long day
of riding the range (or whatever it was
they did in those days) but now

just sort of zenning-out on the back stairs
of a fourth-floor, attic apartment
beneath a black sky all lit up with stars,

sixty some-odd degrees out here
with the odd car *vroom-vroom-vrooming* by
down on the street,

a respectable breeze keeping things
moving about, nicely, and a train moaning out
its woeful long-gone-lonesomeness somewhere
southwest of here,

Nina Simone doing *Do I Move You?*
on the radio (perched precariously
in the kitchen window),
another beer officially *down*
(with four more to go),

a half-pint of apricot brandy
(from Maraska, Croatia, by the way
and how it got here, I'll never know),

a book of classical Chinese poetry
(translated by the criminally underrated
and, seemingly, lost and forgotten
Kenneth Rexroth),

everything boxed up and ready
to load in the morning,

and always, that (hopefully
more than a fool's) hope
that things will go

a little differently

from now on.

Lone Wolves, Black Sheep and Red-Headed Stepchildren

Somewhere,
an empty Mountain Dew bottle
sitting on a limestone fence post
suddenly begins to wheeze and moan
in sweet country harmony
with the wind's sad cowboy song.

Somewhere,
a stiff suburban mummy
stares blankly into his
2,751st consecutive hour
of television;

no one has come calling in years,
no one has noticed the slight,
sickly sweet odor of wasted irony.

Somewhere, the placid dreams
of a dethroned beauty queen
are stirred by the thought of stars
that died a million years ago
whose light is just now reaching us.

And just before dawn,
we'll all be drawn up from
the fathomless well of sleep

to come face to face
with the mongrel faces
of the real *We*,

the prodigal,
near-primordial hybrid
of the lone wolf,
the black sheep
and the red-headed
stepchild

of which
so many,
half-jokingly,
half-nervously speak.

Wherein Our Hero Comes to the Undeniable Conclusion That He's Had Too Much Coffee (or Meditations on Love, Sex, Death, Etc.)
for Adam Mersmann

The sun is fading out
and the streetlights are phasing in
and it looks like another
lonely Sunday night
has rolled around on
The Universal Roulette Wheel again,

another lonely, tight-lipped,
cold-shouldered,
keep-you-at-arm's-length
kind of a night

where nothing in your little corner
of the world seems right
and theres no one around to talk to,
nothing decent to eat or drink in the fridge,
nothing but bad news on the TV and the radio
and not a single, silvery jingle of a ring
from the telephone all night.

And the time is takin its sweet time,
goin nowhere slow and I guess I can say the same
'cause there's really nowhere you can go and nothing to do
with only ten dollars to your name,

snakes in your belly,
high-octane surgin' through your veins
and a batty lone-gunman runnin' round your bell tower
makin' all kinds o' threats and outrageous demands.

So, just what is this nameless, motherless,
coldly-sweating thing, you might ask,
(this time) wearing tights
and a Mexican wrestling mask,
always looming and slavering at us
from just inside the shadows,

this thing that so many of us, so often,
must go toe-to-toe with and take to task
whenever the world suddenly goes cold
and you find yourself alone,
just sitting there in a kitchen
beneath a bare, sixty-watt bulb
or a windowless basement bedroom,
and the TV and the radio are going on and on
about floods and bombs and toxic waste
and a million other variations
of encroaching doom.

Well, maybe any minute now
the phone is gonna sing-out a *hey buddy,
how ya been* kinda song or maybe
a hundred dollar bill is gonna come wafting along
on a gust of cosmic / karmic wind (via your
sock drawer or an old coat pocket)

or maybe that girl that just moved in
next door yesterday might come calling
for no reason at all.

Maybe a Playboy playmate
riding a golden wrecking ball
is gonna come crashing through
my living room wall holding a fishbowl-sized,
desert-dry, Beefeater martini.

Maybe my long-lost Uncle Mikey
is gonna show up out of nowhere
on the very bike he (reportedly) died on
with a single-malt scotch and a bag of weed,
his .357 snub-nose and that boogity-boogity
look in his eyes that always scared
the sweet ba-jeeezus outta me.

Yeah, and maybe Shiva or Lao Tze or Ghandi,
Sweet Georgia Brown or motherfuckin' Johnny Cash
is gonna come floating down on a silvery cloud
and show me the shining path
or secret formula to... what?

Enlightenment? Excitement?
Or escape velocity?
Some sort of quasi-transcendental,
semi-existential, emotive experience, maybe?

So, if there's somebody up there listenin',
in the front row or the cheap seats of Cloud 9,
in the attic of the world (or just the walled-off
upstairs closet of my mind),

gimme a lead,
gimme a hint,
gimme a sign.
Gimme a line or two in your
next big-budget production.

I could be *Thug 2* or *Hillbilly At Bar*
or *Man At Bus Stop*
or somethin'.

And maybe turn the heat up a little
while you're at it.

And could you cash this two-party,
outta state check for me, maybe?
Sorry I aint got any I.D.
of who I am or nothin'.

And brother-man,
could you please tell me,

who's a guy gotta sleep with
to get a little love
in this town?

Writing a Poem About Smoking a Pork Butt in the Rain All Day While Smoking a Pork Butt in the Rain All Day and Writing a Poem About...

for Will Leathem

Decided to write a poem
about smoking a pork butt
in the rain all day (yes, while
smoking a pork butt in the
rain all day) and sitting just
inside the open garage, in a
rusty, rickety folding chair,
drinking a beer, listening
to the KU game on an ancient
transistor radio that family lore
holds was handed down from
old Guglielmo Marconi himself
to my great, great grandfather
to my grandfather, to my father
and then to me, and so, here I am,
smoking a pork butt in the rain,
listening to a basketball game
and watching a few birds
joyously splashing around
in a puddle that has formed
in the giant pothole in the drive,
having the time of their little avian lives,
and I'm thinking that at some point
I should probably find a pen

and scrap of paper and get a few lines
down on this slippery little moment
since it too seems to have been handed
to me by whatever grand (and, we can
assume, otherwise random and indifferent)
universal forces at work around us
all the time, whether we know it or not,
and so, as I was saying, here I am,
writing a poem about smoking a pork
butt in the rain all day while *actually*
smoking a pork butt in the rain all day
and writing a poem about smoking
a pork butt in the rain all day while
smoking a pork butt in the rain all day
and writing a poem about smoking a
pork butt in the rain all day when
I suddenly realize I've been trapped
in some kind of anomalous
temporal loop like you read about
sometimes in sci-fi / fantasy novels,
and no way to free myself, it seems,
and then, just as I'm about to really
start *losing mind and mud*, as they say,
from somewhere, someone hollers
that thing done yet!? and the only thing
that bubbles up (from what surely
must be the most unfathomably
deepest depths of me) to the
deceptively placid surface
of the scene
is *huh?*

On the Road With Uncle Walt and Juice Newton

Woke up to the ancient alarm clock radio
blaring next to my head with the latest mayhem
from around the world and the fairly advanced
stages of a Walt Whitman beard (that I swear
wasn't there when I went to bed),
and it's something about *rockets fired
into crowds armed with rocks* and
I'm wondering, suddenly, if today
wouldn't be one of those days better
devoted to carousing around the country
backroads, drinking beer and picking
wildflowers wherever I find them and,
suddenly, I'm there, in a whirlwind
of activity; it has been decided and
enacted, and I'm driving down a
classic American gravel road
with fence posts to the left of me
and telephone poles to the right,
a Stag tallboy between my legs and
Juice Newton's *Playing With the Queen
of Hearts* (of all things) crackling out
of the AM radio oldies channel and
somehow I know all the words (yes, by heart)
and I'm belting it out like I'm in the band
and all I've had for breakfast is half a bagel,

some kind of B-complex vitamin
and a beer, thinking that I really should
get that broken driver's side taillight
fixed one of these days before my luck
finally runs out, and while this is all probably
not very well thought through if not full-on
ill-advised, it's OK because the point is
I'm here and I have become the invisible,
all-seeing eye of the poem (maybe
somebody else's poem, I don't know),
roving about the classically bucolic
American countryside, tethered
to nothing and beholden to no one,
and I'm thinking how I'd love to have
old Uncle Walt in the passenger seat
next to me, singing along to Juice Newton
or hanging his smiling head out of the
window like a golden retriever or
yellow lab, drunk and delirious
on wind and sun, or standing next to me,
laughing like madmen, as we piss
all our worldly cares away
in a roadside ditch with
wildflowers in our hair,
wildflowers in our pockets,
wildflowers in our
fast-approaching,
afternoon nappy-time
dreams.

A Guided Tour of the Seemingly Banal

This old hat has been a home
to many heads that have hung heavy
with woe.

This bottle has only a few golden swallows
of summer left in it. Drink up.

This tin cup, sitting on this cracked
and mossy headstone is somehow
never empty of shadows.

This cowbell, swinging in the wind
from a barbwire fencepost, has been silenced
by the wattle and daub of an empty wasp's nest.

This rickety chair was forced to sit
facing the corner for being naughty
and disobedient in a previous life.

This hobo's patchwork ragbag is stuffed
with the names of things that no longer exist
(for good reason). Probably best not to open it.

This is an old 78 record of a forgotten poet
whistling an unrecognizable tune
in an empty theater that burned down,
mysteriously, decades ago.

This sad and lonesome tuba (always the fat kid
of musical instruments), languishing for twenty years
in a pawnshop window (its memories of high school
marching bands having mostly faded away)
still dreams of one day sitting in with Tom Waits.

This matchbox once belonged to a famous blues
or rock-a-billy singer. They say it could carry
everything he owned.

This dollhouse has a shy, tiny ghost
that haunts its attic.

This is a closet full of skeletons.

This a drawer full of skeleton keys.

This is a receipt for Chinese takeout
folded into an origami unicorn.
If you look close enough, you can see, scrawled there,
the number for a phone booth by the side
of a lonely stretch of Arizona highway.

They say, every now and then, when the proper
cosmic components are properly aligned and at play,
someone will answer.

Closet Full of Skeletons / Belly Full of Gin
with apologies to Ray Harryhausen

I was fine with the Cyclops.

I was cool with the dragon, even.

I was full-on hunky-dory with the giant
two-headed eagle and the iron Kali statue
suddenly coming-to and doing a little
freaky-deaky, whirling dervish / six-armed
scimitar dance of death.

Hell, I didn't really even flinch much
at the big snake with a woman's head where
the goddamn snake's head should have been.

But for some reason, when that grinning troop
of klinkity-klankity skeletons came high-steppin'
out of the closet like it was Mardi Gras at midnight,
I woke up sweating and screaming, Hollywood style,
and swore to Shiva, Yahweh and the Great Earth Mother
that I'd never have microwave burritos and bathtub gin
before bed again.

Amen to that,
brothers and sisters.

MAGA Hats Are Made in China
for Chigger Matthews

All I could make out was something about horses that wouldn't drink being lead to pasture, and lickin' sticks and rollin' stones and broken black cat bones, and life giving you lemons when you thought you were getting lemon meringue pie, and something else about apples falling either too far or not far enough from trees and the daily chore of chipping and chopping away all day at the *unformed block* only to find it fully reformed again in the morning (GODDAMN, I HATE THAT SHIT!), and early birds ultimately being nothing more than food for worms, and a scrawny squirrel in the pot being worth more than two fat rabbits in your dreams, and then something about the Roman Empire not declining and falling in a day, and the journey of a thousand miles beginning at a mole-hill and ending up on a mountain-top, and something vague about Grecian urns and gift horses with hooves in their mouths, and never putting the plow before the mule, and birds of a feather and idle hands and burning bushes and dogs hunting, and something else about poets seizing the day (or having seizures, daily?) and cooks spoiling soup and captains driving boats into the desert and broken clocks being right twice a day, and going south for the winter being good for both the goose and the gander but maybe not so much for the fish that's found itself out of water, and, of course, not being able to find your way out of a forest because of all the trees… but really, good sir, what the deuce does any of this have to do with the price of MAGA hats made in China?

Drunk in a Bar in Qandahar

She had a wicked straight razor for a smile
and rocket fuel for blood.

Her soul was a mighty sunflower stalk
towering from a five-gallon bucket
in which local legend held something
had drowned before she was even born.

She was the absentee landlady
of a half-way house for recovering
adrenaline junkies.

She lived on a steady diet of
martinis, pills and cigarillos.

She had hi-tech security cameras for eyes.

Her pilot light constantly needed to be relit
by whichever man or woman or non-binary
of the moment that she picked up
on her frequent nightly forays / incursions /
reconnaissance missions.

Rumor had it she slept most of the day
on an ancient chaise lounge that Freud
allegedly lost to Jung in a game of Canasta.

Nobody had seen her in a month
of Sunday school classes.

Her father said she was probably
drunk in a bar in Qandahar or
dead in a ditch in Mogadishu.

But still, every night in my lonely,
fourth-floor attic apartment,
I'd put on my headphones and fire up
my H.A.M. radio, hoping to catch
even the faintest trace
of her flickering
phantom
frequency.

Pitchforks and Tikki Torches (or, How's This for First Thought / Best Thought, Pt.4?)

The night started out with pitchforks and tikki torches (by God we were gonna storm the mad scientist's castle this time!) only to be derailed (again!) with empty platitudes and assuasions and cheap bottles of brandy genrously dispensed about and then, the next thing I know, I'm tumbling headbone over footbone through the pan-o-ramic, psych-o-delic dream-o-sphere for what felt like years and years, only to wake from it all with a scream, sprawled-out on a broken-down couch on the curb of an abandoned suburban Mcmansion in some alternate dystopian version of our own reality. Somehow I'd evaded the ever-watchful electronic eyes of the roving neighborhood robot patrol. Thank God for my paste-on moustache and my dime store wig, and an extra hi-five and *hallelujah* to all the better angels and demons of His (or Her) supernature for giving me the gift of my preternatural Spidey senses, that very instant enabling me to instinctually circumnavigate what must have been a pop bottle Molotov full of piss, thrown from a speeding car of degenerate punks. Little rat fuck bastards. Don't think I didn't get their scent and their license plate number, as well. They'll be feeding the weeds in my backyard this time next week. *Shiiiit,* those mothertruckers must be trippin,' thinkin' I don't know my Queen from my Zeppelin (the point being, keyboards, like any spice or seasoning, are best applied sparingly). But what was it you were saying again, my dear? Something about a treasure map hidden inside a wooden leg?

Uncle Mikey's Hard Night, Out the Door, No Time for Breakfast, Breakfast of Champions

1 highball glass (etched with valiant fisherman wrestling bass or flock of ducks suddenly taking flight).

1 can of beer (Hamms, Olympia, PBR or Stag).

2 raw eggs (chicken, duck or goose. There will most likely be a few trace elements of mud, shit and straw).

1 bottle of hot sauce (Frank's Red Hot, Cholula, Sriracha. Whatever you got).

Pour beer in glass. Let the head die down.

Crack eggs into beer. Watch out for bits of shell (as well as the aforementioned mud, shit and straw).

Add four or five healthy shakes of hot sauce.

Do not mix or stir.

Kill it quick.

Now scoot.

A Few Finer Plot Points
You May Have Missed

What about the rocking chair
on the front porch of the old sanitarium,
rocking back and forth with a ghost
of the wind's nervous energy?

What about the simmering pot
of who knows what left unattended
on the stove for who knows how long?

What about the ancient night-watchman
making his rounds through the collective
dream world of whoever may be sleeping
at any given moment?

What about the lone gypsy prince
wearing Picasso's hat and Dali's mustache,
barreling down I-70 at midnight on his
magnificent chrome machine?

What about bouquets of weeds and wildflowers
as metaphors for any occasion?

What about the meek little man
answering his master's call with
Queen to Bishop6. Checkmate, I think?

What about the haunted player-piano,
spontaneously erupting, now and then,
with Chopin's mazurkas and W.C. Handy's
stomps and boogies (and even the occasional
Gilbert and Sullivan)?

What about the glass eye, possessed by
the spirit of its previous owner, waiting
for the right person to come along?

What about the bluebird trapped
in the boarded-up warehouse,
fluttering frantically for a way out?

What about the bottle-rocket shot by
the tow-headed kid in the first act,
that has apparently been smoldering all this time
on the wood shingle roof of the Pentecostal church?

What about the vacuum left by
the frequent and conspicuous absence
of hope (that red-headed, hair-lipped
little stepchild of the world) just
when it's needed the most?

What about the bride without a head?

What about the lone wolf without a foot?

That Which Doesn't Kill You

still fucks
you up,
nice and
proper,
leaving you
for dead (or
good as)
by the side
of a road,
or at the
bottom of
an abandoned
rock quarry,
or in a burning
warehouse
down by
the docks,
whatever;
then, years later,
begins to
call you
on the phone
every now and
then, in the
middle of

of Christmas
dinner, your
birthday, your
20th anniversary,
whatever,
just to tell you
that it
could have
sent you
to a deep
dark place
from which
there is
no return
(if'n it really
wanted to),
so you
better
watch
your ass,
punk.
*Oh, and
hey, how's
the wife
and
kids?*

Integer Line

The $5 black
wrap-around
truckstop sunglasses
were minding their
own business, resting
next to the mysterious
brown paper bag
which had just been
delivered that very
moment by the
tongue-less dwarf
(with the bright
jungle bird on his
shoulder) and
contained, much to
our surprise, a single
chess piece (a queen,
by the way) and
a set of keys that
looked like a
glittering undersea
creature when
splayed-out on
the spacious dining
room table before us
and catching the light
from a lamp in the corner,
radiating out its

golden, narcotic glow,
like a halo above the
conspicuously dapper man,
sitting in the over-
stuffed chair beneath it
(with the stuffing
and even a few springs
coming out, here
and there), a cup
of tea steaming
on the end table
next to him,
an open pocketknife
in one hand, a yellow
Ticonderoga
pencil in the other,
his attention focused,
eagerly and earnestly,
on something visible
only to him,
situated exactly
in the middle
of the integer line
that spanned
the distance
between
those two
points.

Asking for a Friend

Not to cling too tightly to
old-fashioned notions about things,

but is it the slightest bit weird if a
standard issue *cis-het* / gender-normative-
type guy has accumulated, over the years,
a shoebox of what you might call *oddments*
or *mementos* that had each been,
either, carelessly discarded or freely given,

but still, no doubt long forgotten the minute
they were out of the sight and minds
of the various women, over the years, who
this dude (this rube, this hayseed, this semi-
loveable schmoe) had been so damn sure
(at the time, anyway) were specifically
fated and designated *(I know, I know)* for him
and he, likewise, for them, as well (and *all* that jive):

as in *made for each other,* as in *perfect for*
(as they use to say in what, surely, must have been
a slightly less cynical age than our own),

and still sometimes seems that way
whenever he gets a good, lonesome drunk on
and starts pining over this box full of junk
that somehow manages to resurface
from time to time, because he won't
just get rid of it finally FOR FUCK SAKE...

And him just sitting there,
listening to some God-awful maudlin music in the dark,
slowly turning himself on a spit over a low blue flame,
ping-ponging his mushy, late middle-aged brain,
back and forth, between the opposing polarities
of The Way He Remembers Things Happening
Way Back When and What Could Have Been,
maybe? / possibly? / if only things had
played out any other way
than the way they did.

But they didn't.
And that's that.

Before he was even
out of the gate
it was too little,
too late, too bad.

And there ain't
no do-overs,
and there ain't
no come-backs.

Jason Ryberg is the author of sixteen books of poetry, six screenplays, a few short stories, several angry letters to various magazine and newspaper editors, and a box full of folders, notebooks and scraps of paper that could one day be (loosely) construed as a novel. He is currently an artist-in-residence at both The Prospero Institute of Disquieted P/o/e/t/i/c/s and the Osage Arts Community. He lives part-time in Kansas City with a rooster named Little Red and a billygoat named Giuseppe and part-time somewhere in the Ozarks, near the Gasconade River, where there are also many strange and wonderful woodland critters.

www.ingramcontent.com/pod-product-compliance
Lightning Source LLC
Chambersburg PA
CBHW030119100526
44591CB00009B/452